■ SCHOLASTIC

Hi-Lo Passages
TO BUILD
Comprehension

Grades 5–6
by Michael Priestley

New York • Toronto • London • Auckland • Sydney
Mexico City • New Delhi • Hong Kong • Buenos Aires

Teaching Resources

Cover design by Maria Lilja
Interior design by Creative Pages, Inc.
Interior illustrations by Yvette Banet pages 9, 17, 20, 32; Ka Botzis, page 22; Eva Vagreti Cockrille, pages 26 & 27, 44 & 45; Drew-Brook-Cormack, page 40; Jennifer Emery, page 28; Kathleen Kemly, page 19; Neecy Twinem, page 13.

ISBN: 0-439-54888-8

9 10   40   11 12 13 14 15 /C

Hi-Lo Passages to Build Comprehension

Grades 5–6

Contents

A Note for Teachers

Reading is the key to learning, and today's students read materials from an ever-increasing number of sources. They must understand what they read in traditional forms of fiction and nonfiction, such as stories and news articles. They must also comprehend newer forms of text, such as advertisements on Web sites and e-mail on the Internet. Many students can benefit from more practice in reading, but finding good examples of hi-lo texts for instruction at the appropriate grade level can be challenging.

How to Use This Book

The main purpose of this book is to provide high-interest passages for students to read. All the passages in this book are intended to be motivating and interesting, but they are written at a lower grade level. You can find the readability score for each passage in the table of contents. (Both Spache and Dale-Chall scoring criteria were used in determining readability level.) These passages can be used for practice and instruction in reading, and they can be used to help prepare students for taking tests. Most important, they can help students enjoy what they read.

This book provides 25 passages in a wide variety of genres, including informational articles, letters, biographies, web pages, and how-to guides. The passages (of one to two pages) focus on high-interest topics and comprehension skills, such as making inferences or comparing and contrasting. Passages have three or five comprehension questions based on the skills. The questions are intended mainly to help students think about what they have read. (If you want to check student responses, you may refer to the Answer Key at the back of the book.)

These questions will also help you assess students' comprehension of the material and will help students practice answering test questions. Questions include multiple-choice items and short-answer items. Some of the passages include writing prompts to elicit longer responses.

Extending Activities

For some of these passages, you may want to have students go beyond answering the questions that are provided. For example, for any given passage you could have students write a summary of the selection in their own words or rewrite the passage from a different point of view. For some pairs of texts, you might have students compare and contrast the two selections. For other passages, you might want to create writing prompts and have students write full-length essays about what they have learned. Students will benefit from reading and analyzing these passages, discussing them in class or in small groups, and writing about them in a variety of ways.

Passage 1   Making Inferences and Predictions

Snow Day

Tom could hardly wait for morning. Snow was falling swiftly. By morning he anticipated that there would be enough snow to make a great snowman.

Tom had never made a snowman before. He had just moved to Indiana from Alabama, where it hardly ever snowed.

The next morning, Tom's mother shook him gently. "No school today," she said. "There's too much snow for the school bus to get through."

Tom let out a whoop. He jumped out of bed and pulled on his snow clothes. His snow pants swished and his boots clomped as he walked toward the door.

Tom's friends, Herb and Addie, were already outside. "Hey, Tom!" called Addie. "We're going to Warwick Hill in a little while. Do you want to come?"

"Not now," Tom answered. "I'm going to make a snowman."

Herb shook his head. "This isn't snowman snow, Tom," he said. "It's too dry and fluffy." Herb shoved his mittens into the snow and scooped some up. Then he puffed up his cheeks and exhaled. The snow scattered like dust.

Tom looked down at the ground. Snow was snow, he'd always thought. How was he supposed to know there were different kinds? "What kind of snow is this?" he asked.

"It's sledding snow!" chuckled Addie. "That's why we're going to Warwick Hill. All the kids will be there, and you should come, too." Addie held a sled out to Tom and said, "You can use this. We've got two more."

Tom took the sled and grinned. After all, he'd never been sledding before.

1. When Tom lets out a whoop, how do you think he feels?

    Ⓐ hurt   Ⓒ mad

    Ⓑ happy   Ⓓ cold

2. How do you think Tom feels when he looks down at the ground?

    Ⓐ foolish   Ⓒ bored

    Ⓑ glad   Ⓓ proud

3. What will Tom probably do next?

_____

Passage 2   Comparing and Contrasting

Hopping Around the World

Hopscotch is a very old game. It usually uses a puck, such as a stone, and a pattern that players hop through. Here are different versions to play.

Scotch-Hoppers

Children in England and Scotland play this game with a stone. Throw the stone into Box 1. Hop over Box 1 and through the pattern. On the way back, hop into Box 1, pick up the stone, and hop out. Then, toss the puck into Box 2, and so on. If your stone enters the wrong box, start over! The first player to throw the stone into each box and hop through the whole pattern wins.

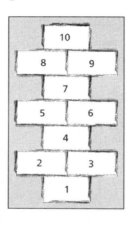

Escargot *Escargot* is the French word for "snail." For this game, the pattern looks like a snail. No puck is used. Players hop through the pattern on one foot. You may rest in the center on both feet. After resting, hop back through the pattern and out. If you finish the pattern without stepping on a line, write your name in a space. No other player may land in that space. At the end, the player who owns the most spaces wins.

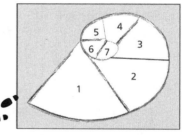

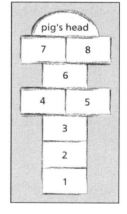

Pele Children play Pele on the island of Aruba with a stone or coin. Throw the puck into the first box and hop into Box 2. Next, hop up to the top of the pattern and turn around. Then, come back to Box 2, and pick up the puck in Box 1. Hop over Box 1 and out of the pattern. Next, throw the puck into Box 2 and start again. If you make a mistake, you lose your turn. The first player to hop through the pattern wins.

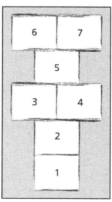

Gat Fei Gei In this Chinese version of hopscotch, the puck is a piece of roof tile. At the top is the pig's head. Toss the puck into the pig's head and hop through the pattern. When you reach boxes 7 and 8, spin around and pick up the puck from behind. If you hop through the pattern without making a mistake, pick a box and write your name in it. No one else can land in that box! The player who owns the most boxes wins.

La Thunkuña Children play this game in Bolivia, a country in South America. The puck is a stone or the peel from an orange. Instead of writing a number in each square, players write each day of the week. Throw the puck into the first box. Hop over it into the second box. Next, kick the puck backwards and out of the pattern. Then, hop out. On your next turn, throw the puck into the next space, and so on. The first player to hop all the way through wins.

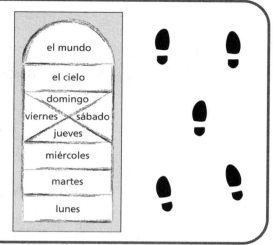

1. **Name two ways in which Escargot is different from all the other games.**

   _____

   _____

2. **How are the board squares for La Thunkuña different from the board squares in the other games?**

   _____

   _____

3. **In which two games do winners get to "own" spaces?**
   - Ⓐ La Thunkuña and Scotch-Hoppers
   - Ⓑ Pele and Escargot
   - Ⓒ Scotch-Hoppers and Gat Fei Gei
   - Ⓓ Gat Fei Gei and Escargot

4. **Which is the only game that uses an orange peel for a puck?**
   - Ⓐ Scotch-Hoppers
   - Ⓑ La Thunkuña
   - Ⓒ Pele
   - Ⓓ Gat Fei Gei

5. **Which two games show animals in the gameboard?**
   - Ⓐ Gat Fei Gei and Escargot
   - Ⓑ Pele and La Thunkuña
   - Ⓒ Scotch-Hoppers and Escargot
   - Ⓓ La Thunkuña and Scotch-Hoppers

Passage 3   Comparing and Contrasting

Problems Solved-By Kids!

On a winter day in 1873, Chester Greenwood went ice skating in Maine. It was a very cold day. But Chester skated with a bare head. He didn't want to wrap a wool scarf around his head. Wool made Chester itch! Soon, Chester's ears were so cold they hurt.

Chester had an idea for keeping his ears warm. He told his grandmother about it. Together they made two ear coverings from fur and cloth. Then they connected them to a wire. They shaped the wire to fit Chester's head so that his ears would stay warm. That's how the first earmuffs were invented!

Before long the idea of earmuffs caught on. Chester Greenwood opened an earmuff factory and became a rich man.

About 100 years later, Suzanna Goodin, age 6, had a different problem. Every day she spooned cat food into her cat's bowl. Then she had to wash the spoon. Suzanna didn't like this. She wanted to feed her cat without washing a spoon.

An idea finally came to Suzanna. She asked her grandmother for help. They made some dough and shaped it like a spoon. Next they baked the spoon to make it strong and firm. Suzanna dished out her cat food with the spoon. Then she broke the spoon into pieces and put them in the cat's bowl. On the first try, Suzanna's cat didn't like the taste of the spoon. But Suzanna didn't give up. She changed the recipe to give it a taste her cat liked.

Later Suzanna entered her spoons in a contest–and she won!

1. **How were Chester and Suzanna alike?**
   - Ⓐ Both had pet cats.
   - Ⓑ Both liked to ice skate.
   - Ⓒ Both invented something.
   - Ⓓ Both opened factories.

2. **Both Chester and Suzanna got some help from a _____.**
   - Ⓐ teacher   Ⓒ friend
   - Ⓑ grandmother   Ⓓ brother

3. **Name one way Suzanna Goodin was different from Chester Greenwood.**

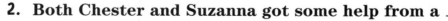

Passage 4   Cause and Effect

Squirrel in a Life Jacket

People of all ages enjoy the sport of water-skiing. So does a squirrel named Twiggy! Twiggy and her owner, Lou Ann Best, go to boat shows in the United States and Europe. At these shows, Twiggy water-skis around a tiny swimming pool. She's pulled by a small toy boat. She wears a tiny red life jacket.

The crowds at the boat shows always laugh and cheer for Twiggy. Lou Ann also wants everyone to learn an important water safety lesson. As Twiggy circles the pool, Lou Ann points out the squirrel's red life jacket. When you go boating or water-skiing, she tells the crowd, always remember to wear a life jacket.

Lou Ann Best has been in the boat show business since 1978. That's when a friend gave a baby squirrel to Lou Ann and her husband, Chuck. The squirrel had been hurt during a storm. Lou Ann and Chuck fed and cared for the squirrel. They named it Twiggy. Once Twiggy was healthy, Chuck decided to teach her to water-ski. How did he get such an idea? Chuck had already trained other animals—ponies, dogs, and a toad—to do the same thing. Before long, the Bests were showing off their squirrel on water skis at boat shows.

After a few years, the Bests decided to let Twiggy stop working. They fixed up a special room in their house for her. They covered the floor with plant material. Then they added lots of tree branches. But Chuck and Lou Ann were having too much fun to retire. They trained another squirrel to water-ski. Then another, and another. In all, there have been five squirrels on water skis. Like the first, each one was a baby that needed a home. And each has been named Twiggy.

Sadly, Chuck Best died in 1997. For a while, Lou Ann could not bring herself to do the boat shows without him. But Twiggy was greatly missed. The people who ran the shows kept phoning Lou Ann. They begged her to change her mind.

Finally, Lou Ann gave in. She and the newest Twiggy packed up and headed for the next boat show. Now Lou Ann is glad she's back in show business. When she hears the crowds cheer for Twiggy, she feels happy and proud.

1. Why do crowds laugh and cheer when they see Twiggy?

_____

_____

_____

2. What water safety lesson does the crowd learn as a result of Twiggy's show?

_____

_____

_____

3. Chuck Best believed he could teach Twiggy to water-ski because _____.

 Ⓐ he had already taught other animals to water-ski

 Ⓑ a friend told him it was easy to do

 Ⓒ he had seen squirrels water-ski at boat shows before

 Ⓓ squirrels are good swimmers

4. Why did Lou Ann stop going to the boat shows for a while?

 Ⓐ Twiggy was too old to water-ski.

 Ⓑ People weren't interested in seeing Twiggy anymore.

 Ⓒ She didn't want to go after her husband died.

 Ⓓ The crowds at the boat shows frightened Twiggy.

5. What makes Lou Ann Best feel happy and proud?

_____

_____

_____

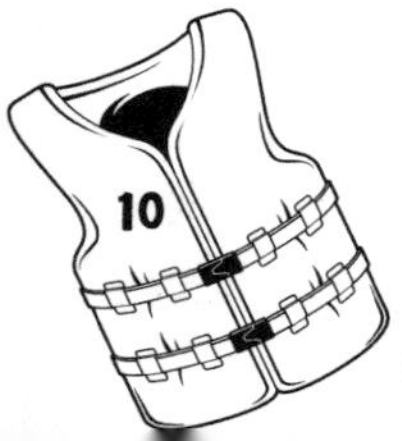

Passage 5   Sequence/Steps in a Process

Don't Bake These Cookies!

Cookies made at home always taste better than cookies purchased from a store. But measuring, mixing, and baking are a lot of work! Here's a recipe for some great cookies you don't have to bake. What could be better than that? Don't make this recipe if you can't eat peanuts. And make sure to have a grown-up help you.

Ingredients
1/2 cup milk
2 cups sugar
1 stick butter

1 teaspoon vanilla
1/2 cup peanut butter
2 tablespoons cocoa
3 cups dry oatmeal

Steps
1. Put the sugar, butter, and milk in a cooking pot. Mix them together.
2. *Ask a grown-up for help with this step.* Cook the mixture on the stove. Stir as it cooks. When the mixture starts to bubble, cook and stir for one minute more.
3. Remove the pot from the stove. Add the vanilla and stir.
4. Put the mixture into a large bowl. Add the peanut butter, cocoa, and oatmeal. Stir everything together.
5. Put some wax paper on a cookie sheet. Place spoonfuls of the cookie mixture on the wax paper. Then let the cookies cool for 30 minutes.

Once the cookies have cooled, you can eat them. They taste delicious with a glass of milk!

1. **Which three ingredients should you mix together first?**

_____

2. **After you remove the pot from the stove, what should you do next?**
   - Ⓐ Ask a grown-up for help.
   - Ⓑ Wait for the mixture to bubble.
   - Ⓒ Add the vanilla and stir.
   - Ⓓ Add the cocoa.

3. **What should you do after you put spoonfuls of the cookie mixture on wax paper?**

_____

Passage 6   Main Idea and Details

A Brother in the Band

Not long ago, a rock band called the Backstreet Boys made a big splash on the music scene. Young people everywhere loved their songs. One of the band's biggest fans was a young boy named Aaron Carter. Aaron had a special reason for taking such an interest in the band. Nick Carter, one of the Backstreet Boys, was Aaron's big brother.

Even before Nick joined the band in 1996, Aaron loved music. From the age of two, Aaron spent lots of time listening to the radio. He sang along with his favorite songs. He made up dances to go with them. That's why Aaron's family was not surprised when Aaron decided to follow Nick into the music world.

Aaron got off to a fast start. At the age of seven, he joined a band in his hometown of Tampa, Florida. But after two years, Aaron didn't want to be part of a band anymore. He wanted to sing alone. Soon, brother Nick gave Aaron a helping hand. During a Backstreet Boys show in Germany, Aaron sang a song. He did an amazing job! After the show, someone from a record company asked Aaron to make an album. Of course, Aaron said yes!

Since that day, Aaron has made hit after hit. His songs include "Crush on You" and "I'm Gonna Miss You Forever."

Aaron has worked hard to become a success. But he never forgets how his brother gave him his start. As Aaron has said, "If Nick wasn't a singer, then I wouldn't be here."

1. Who is Aaron Carter?

_____

_____

2. Backstreet Boys is the name of a _____.
    Ⓐ play   Ⓒ movie
    Ⓑ band   Ⓓ song

3. How did Nick Carter help his brother get started?
    Ⓐ He made up some dances for Aaron.
    Ⓑ He wrote some songs for Aaron's first album.
    Ⓒ He let Aaron sing a song during a show in Germany.
    Ⓓ He told Aaron to listen to the radio and sing along.

Passage 7   Main Idea and Details

A Fascinating Fish

How did the sea horse get its name? It's not hard to guess. The top half of this fish looks like a small horse. But looking at the sea horse's long, curled tail, you might think "sea monkey" is a more accurate name. Then there's the sea horse's pouch, which is used for carrying eggs until they hatch. "Sea kangaroo" might also be an appropriate name for this fish.

Sea horses live in warm ocean waters all over the world. There are 32 different kinds of sea horses. They range in size from one inch long to about one foot long. Because their fins are small, sea horses swim extremely slowly. They keep safe from other fish by hiding in plants and grasses that grow beneath the sea. They can also change colors to blend in with their surroundings. A sea horse remains in one place for hours at a time by winding its tail around a plant. It feeds on live food, such as tiny shrimp, that happen to swim by. A sea horse has no teeth, so it swallows the shrimp whole. For a fish that doesn't move around much, the sea horse eats a lot. In just one day, a sea horse can eat 3,000 shrimp!

A sea horse keeps the same mate for its whole life, unlike most kinds of fish. And it's the male sea horse, not the female, which gives birth to baby sea horses. How does this happen? Baby sea horses start out as eggs, which come from the female's body. But the female places the eggs in the male sea horse's pouch. The male carries the eggs for about three weeks until they hatch. Soon after the babies are born, the female gives her mate a new set of eggs. The male sea horse spends most of its life carrying eggs.

Some people worry that sea horses may be in trouble. The number of sea horses is becoming smaller. Why is this happening? Some places where sea horses once lived have been filled in to make new land. Also, many sea horses are caught and sold as aquarium fish. This really is not a good idea because most sea horses don't live long in aquariums. The best place for a sea horse is the ocean. There it can find a mate and bring new sea horses into the world.

1. **What is this article mostly about?**
   - Ⓐ animal names
   - Ⓑ sea horses
   - Ⓒ aquariums
   - Ⓓ oceans

2. **How does a sea horse keep safe from other fish?**

   _____

   _____

3. **What does a female sea horse do with her eggs?**

   _____

   _____

4. **Why is the number of sea horses becoming smaller?**

   _____

   _____

5. **Which is another good title for this article?**
   - Ⓐ "Animal Fathers"
   - Ⓑ "Kinds of Horses"
   - Ⓒ "How Fish Grow"
   - Ⓓ "All About Sea Horses"

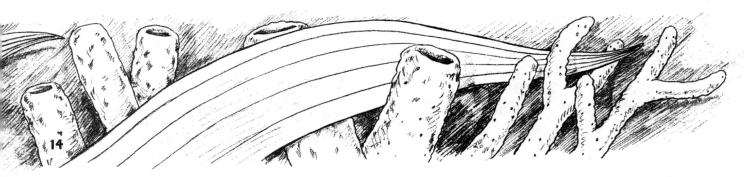

Passage 8   Author's Purpose and Point of View

A Delicious Mistake

Every day, people invent new things. Some inventors work hard for years to create something new. But some of the best inventions happen by accident.

Can you imagine a world without chocolate chip cookies? Back in 1930, Ruth Wakefield and her husband opened a restaurant in Massachusetts. It was called the Toll House Inn. Ruth greeted the guests when they arrived. She also worked as the cook. The restaurant held 30 guests. Ruth often had to rush to feed them all on time.

One day, Ruth was mixing up some chocolate cookies in the kitchen. The recipe said to melt squares of baking chocolate. The next step was to pour the melted chocolate into the pale cookie batter and stir.

You have to melt chocolate slowly or it will burn. Ruth was in a hurry. She decided to break the chocolate squares into little chunks. Then she threw the chunks into the batter. After all, the cookies had to bake in a hot oven. She figured that the chocolate would just melt into the rest of the batter.

When she took the cookies out of the oven, Ruth groaned. She could still see big chunks of chocolate. She could never serve these to her guests!

Then, Ruth tasted the cookies. They were delicious! Her guests agreed.

Ruth began buying lots of chocolate and cutting it up. Then she asked the candy makers if they could make the chocolate easier to break into small pieces. That's when they came up with chocolate chips. If it were really easy to make these delicious cookies, maybe people would start baking them at home.

Thanks to Ruth Wakefield, today you can find "Toll House" cookies in every grocery store. But none of them tastes as good as a homemade chocolate chip cookie, hot from the oven.

1. **The author's main purpose in writing this article was to _____.**
   - (A) teach how to make chocolate chip cookies
   - (B) explain how to become an inventor
   - (C) describe how chocolate chip cookies were first made
   - (D) tell about the life of Ruth Wakefield

2. **What does the author think about chocolate chip cookies?**
   - (A) They are good.
   - (B) Most kinds are boring.
   - (C) They taste bad.
   - (D) They are neither good or bad.

3. **What does the author most likely think about Ruth Wakefield and her invention?**
   - (A) She was lucky.
   - (B) She was very smart.
   - (C) She was silly.
   - (D) She was a bad cook.

4. **How do you think the author feels about the candy makers who decided to make chocolate chips?**

   _____

   _____

5. **Which kind of chocolate chip cookie does the author think tastes the best?**

   _____

   _____

Writing Prompt: **Write a speech for your class. Tell how you feel about chocolate chip cookies.**

Scholastic Teaching Resources   **Grades 5-6**

Passage 9   Story Elements

The Amazing Angie

Angie spied the old flower vase on a shelf in the basement. It was made of glass and was nearly as round as a ball. "I wonder what I can do with this," Angie said. She carried the vase up to the kitchen and rinsed the dust off of it.

Just then there was a knock at the front door. Angie opened it and saw her neighbor, Mr. Leopold. "Is your brother home?" he asked.

"No, Corey's at a friend's house," replied Angie.

"Well, when he gets home, please ask him to come see me. I've noticed what a fine job he does mowing your lawn, and I'd like him to mow my lawn every week. I'll pay him, of course."

"All right," said Angie, "I'll send him over."

"And by the way, I noticed your dad's car has a flat tire."

Angie looked past Mr. Leopold. Sure enough, one of the back tires on Dad's car was flat.

Just then the phone rang. "Excuse me, Mr. Leopold," Angie said, as she closed the door and ran to the phone.

"Angie, this is Mrs. Verrier. Can I speak to your mom?"

"She's still at work," Angie replied.

"Just have her give me a call later," said Mrs. Verrier. "I have a huge surprise for her."

"Can you tell me what it is?" asked Angie.

"I just got tickets for the two of us to go to the Bruce Springsteen concert next week," replied Mrs. Verrier.

"Oh, she'll be thrilled!" exclaimed Angie.

"I know, but don't say anything. I want to tell her myself!" said Mrs. Verrier.

As Angie hung up the phone, the round glass vase caught her eye. She examined it for a few minutes, and then a smile spread across her face. "This is going to be fun," Angie said.

With that, Angie ran to her room and pulled on her shiny blue bathrobe. Next she found the scarf she wanted. Angie wrapped the scarf around her head and knotted it at the back of her neck. Then she hurried to her parents' room, found Mom's gold hoop earrings, and clipped them on.

When Angie went downstairs again, her father was getting ready to make dinner. A puzzled look crossed his face when he saw how Angie was dressed.

Angie picked up the vase and held it out in front of her. Then she spun gaily around. "When will Mom and Corey be home, Dad?" she asked.

"Any minute. Why?"

"Well," laughed Angie, "when everyone's here, I, the Amazing Angie, am going to tell your future!"

1. Where is Angie in the beginning of this story?
- Ⓐ in the basement
- Ⓑ in the kitchen
- Ⓒ in the driveway
- Ⓓ at a friend's house

2. Mr. Leopold comes to Angie's house to _____.
- Ⓐ mow the lawn
- Ⓑ sell concert tickets
- Ⓒ fix Dad's flat tire
- Ⓓ offer Corey a job

3. Mrs. Verrier has a huge surprise for _____.
- Ⓐ Angie
- Ⓑ Angie's mother
- Ⓒ Corey
- Ⓓ Angie's father

4. What does Angie decide to do with the vase?

_____

_____

_____

5. How does Angie feel at the end of the story?
- Ⓐ excited
- Ⓑ worried
- Ⓒ puzzled
- Ⓓ foolish

Name _____ Date _____

The Show Must Go On!

The doctor examined Nuala's leg. Nuala tried not to cry, but it was a challenge. Her leg really ached.

"How did you hurt yourself?" asked the doctor.

"I jumped off a swing," said Nuala. "Is it broken?"

"It sure is," said the doctor, holding out the X ray. "See right here?"

Two hours later, Nuala left the hospital on crutches. Her leg was in a cast.

"What will I tell Ms. Chang?" she asked her mother in the car.

Ms. Chang was Nuala's dance teacher. The spring dance performance was only two weeks away. Nuala's cast would be on for at least six weeks!

"She's going to be so mad at me!" groaned Nuala.

But Ms. Chang wasn't mad. She said, "We'll think of something."

Nuala felt ridiculous going on stage with her crutches. "I look stupid," she complained. "I can't dance with these."

"Have you ever heard the expression, 'The show must go on'?" said Ms. Chang. Together, they went through the show. They thought of how Nuala could move to the music. They brainstormed ways for her to dance on crutches.

The night of the performance, Ms. Chang almost had to push Nuala on the stage. Nuala's cast looked big and clumsy, but she went out and danced. At the end, the audience went wild clapping. Someone tossed a bouquet of roses at Nuala's feet! The show did go on!

1. Where does the first part of the story take place?

_____

2. What is Nuala's problem?

_____

3. What lesson can be learned from this story?
- Ⓐ Never ride on a swing.
- Ⓑ Don't try to do two things at once.
- Ⓒ The only things worth doing are those that take hard work.
- Ⓓ If you work together, you can overcome problems.

Passage 11   Sequence

The Last Day

The classroom was buzzing with excitement. When Mr. Brinks walked in carrying a CD player, everyone grinned. We knew we were going to have fun.

"Settle down, everyone. Take your seats," called Mr. Brinks. Then he looked around the room and added, "I'm glad everyone's here for the last spelling test of the year." He picked up some writing paper, as if he were going to pass it out. When everyone groaned, Mr. Brinks laughed. "Just kidding," he said. "But really, we have some work to do."

"What?" we all asked at once. It was the last day of school. No one was planning to work.

"You need to clean out your desks. Turn in your books to me and put everything else into your backpacks." With that, Mr. Brinks plugged in the CD player and turned it on.

The music created a party mood. Some of us sang along, and some of us danced around our desks as we cleaned them out. Mr. Brinks did a few fancy steps as he cleared off the bulletin board. Everyone laughed. It was a side of Mr. Brinks we didn't see very often.

When our desks were clean, someone asked, "How long until recess?" Mr. Brinks opened the closet and pulled out three balls. He tossed them into the air and started juggling them around and around. Then he let the balls drop and roll across the floor. "Recess starts . . . now!" he cried.

Just then Mrs. Molinas, the principal, stuck her head into the room. "Mr. Brinks!" she exclaimed.

The room fell silent. Everyone was looking at Mrs. Molinas. We were afraid Mr. Brinks was in big trouble now. But Mrs. Molinas's mouth was wiggling. She was trying to look annoyed, but she couldn't do it. Finally, she broke out laughing and walked away down the hall.

Mr. Brinks took us outside for the rest of recess. After recess, Mr. Brinks led us back into the school. On the way to our room, he stopped at the lunchroom. "I just need to get something from the freezer," he explained. Then he pulled out three boxes of ice cream.

"All right!" we said. "Hurray for Mr. Brinks!"

As we followed him down the hall toward our classroom, we passed Mrs. Molinas' office. "Don't juggle the ice cream, Mr. Brinks!" one of the kids said, and everyone laughed.

Mr. Brinks laughed the hardest of all.

1. What did Mr. Brinks do first in this story?

_____

_____

_____

2. What happened right after Mr. Brinks told the students to clean their desks, turn in their books, and put things into their backpacks?

_____

_____

_____

3. While the students cleaned their desks, Mr. Brinks _____.

- Ⓐ handed out books to the students
- Ⓑ cleared off the bulletin board and danced
- Ⓒ took some balls out of the closet
- Ⓓ went to get something from the lunchroom

4. What happened just before Mrs. Molinas stuck her head into the classroom?

_____

_____

_____

5. What happened last in this story?

- Ⓐ Mr. Brinks juggled the ice cream.
- Ⓑ Mr. Brinks led his class out to recess.
- Ⓒ Mr. Brinks got in trouble with the principal.
- Ⓓ Mr. Brinks and his students laughed.

Passage 12   Author's Purpose and Point of View

What's in a Name?

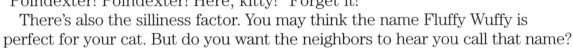

Choosing a name for a pet is a big responsibility! After all, a name lasts for life.

A pet's name should be easy to say, especially if the animal will go outside. For example, Poindexter is kind of cute. But imagine standing at the back door calling, "Poindexter! Poindexter! Here, kitty!" Forget it!

There's also the silliness factor. You may think the name Fluffy Wuffy is perfect for your cat. But do you want the neighbors to hear you call that name?

Some people give their pets people names, like Sam or Winnie. This can really make the dog or cat seem like one of the family, but it can cause some problems. What if your dog and your best friend are both called Sam? Your friend might get upset if he hears you yell, "Sit, Sam!"

Many people's names have old meanings that can be interesting. If you decide to use a name that means something, try to pick one that fits the animal. The name Megan would not fit a tiny, fluffy cat. In Greek it means "big, strong one"! Maybe you could use it for a German Shepherd.

One of the best ways find a name is to look in a name book. These books tell the meanings of names. Then when your family buys an Irish setter with long red hair, you will know what to name her: Rooney! That's Irish for "red one." Your black cat can be Layla. That means "dark as the night."

Baggins

Bessie

Ninja
Opal

1. **The author of this article wants people to _____.**
   - Ⓐ get more pets
   - Ⓑ let kids name their baby sisters and brothers
   - Ⓒ pick good names for pets
   - Ⓓ take better care of their animals

2. **What is one of the best ways to pick a name, according to the author?**

   _____

3. **The author wrote this article mainly to _____.**
   - Ⓐ give information about names
   - Ⓑ teach a lesson about pets
   - Ⓒ compare different kinds of pets
   - Ⓓ talk about families

Seymour

Gracie
Abner
Ajax
Zippy
Pandora

Gita

Periwinkle
Maggie
Merlin Nemo

Ozzie

22

Passage 13   Cause and Effect

Ask Daisy

Dear Daisy,

I read your advice for kids in the newspaper every day. Your answers often help me with my own problems. But I've never seen a letter about the problem I've got now. That's why I'm writing!

My problem is my best friend. His name is Vic, and he's really great. He's kind and funny, and I can always count on him when I need help. But Vic doesn't want me to have any friends besides him! When I make plans with someone else, Vic acts surprised and hurt. Then I end up getting mad at him!

I still want to be best friends with Vic, but I want to have other friends, too. Please tell me what I should do.

Leon

Dear Leon,

Start by telling Vic what you told me. He's your best friend, and you don't want that to change. Vic may be worried that you'll make a new best friend and forget all about him. Let him know that's not true.

You can also try to include Vic when you make plans with other friends. Maybe he'll join in, and your friends will become his friends, too. But if he doesn't want to, don't push him. Some kids prefer to have just one or two really good friends, and there's nothing wrong with that.

Daisy

1. **Leon needs advice from Daisy because he _____.**
   - Ⓐ has too many friends
   - Ⓑ is having trouble with his best friend
   - Ⓒ doesn't want new friends
   - Ⓓ doesn't like his old friends anymore

2. **Why does Leon think Vic is such a great friend?**

   _____

   _____

3. **What does Vic do when Leon makes plans with other friends?**
   - Ⓐ He says he doesn't care.
   - Ⓑ He invites another friend to play.
   - Ⓒ He acts surprised and hurt.
   - Ⓓ He says mean things to Leon.

Passage 14   Making Inferences and Predictions

Letter From the New World

Dear Aunt Anne,

Here we are in the New World. At first the forests seemed dark and empty. Then we saw eyes looking at us from the trees.

We did not want to go too far from our camp. Our leader said that he would look around. When he came back he was laughing. He told us that he had been walking along. Suddenly he was upside down hanging from a tree. It was a trap made by the Indians. They had caught him instead of a deer! Another man cut him down.

We got to know the Indians slowly. We watched how they caught fish. We copied them. They pointed to the plants that were safe to eat. My friends and I had the job of picking fruit. Sometimes we returned with purple lips and fingers. Our pockets were empty. Our parents were angry. The Indians smiled.

We were hungry during the winter. We were farmers and were used to planting big fields of wheat and potatoes. We were used to having cows and plenty of milk.

One spring morning, an Indian arrived. He wanted us to follow him. We came to the top of a hill and looked down. Below were fields. The Indians were farmers, too!

They showed us what they were planting. We had never seen such seeds. They looked like yellow teeth. One man pulled a dead fish out of a basket. He put the fish in a hole. Next he put seeds on top. Then he filled the hole with dirt.

Our Indian friend gave us a small bag. He handed it to us as if it were full of gold! Inside were the yellow "teeth." Our leader thanked the Indians. Then we returned to camp.

"Time to dig!" said our leader. "Time to catch fish, too."

Everyone smiled. Maybe we will have plenty of food soon!

Your loving nephew,
Ephraim

1. **How do the colonists feel when they first see the Indians in the forest?**

   Ⓐ scared

   Ⓑ friendly

   Ⓒ excited

   Ⓓ angry

2. **Why do the children sometimes come back to camp with purple lips?**

   _____

   _____

3. **Why do you think Ephraim's parents were angry?**

   _____

   _____

4. **What do you think the yellow "teeth" are?**

   Ⓐ pieces of cheese

   Ⓑ dried corn

   Ⓒ teeth from fish

   Ⓓ gold bits

5. **What will the colonists probably do next?**

   Ⓐ Have dinner.

   Ⓑ Ask the Indians for food.

   Ⓒ Plant seeds.

   Ⓓ Get some cows.

25

Passage 15   Drawing Conclusions

Piggy Heaven

If you're an English pig, this is your lucky day! A new law says that the farmer who owns you has to keep you healthy and happy.

Now you probably live in an empty pen. It's easy for the farmer to clean, but you have always hated it. It's so dull. Pigs like to sniff around with their noses.

The new law says that you must have something to smell. Maybe it will be some sweet-smelling hay or bits of wood.

And the new law says you need toys, too!

Footballs and other kinds of balls are just the right toys. With many toys, the pigs will not get tired of the same one.

You know what happens when you have nothing to do. You get very mean. You start biting each other. You start chewing each other's ears and tails. Having a nice new football to push around will help you stay happy.

Some farmers say that the new laws are not really needed. They say that their pigs are fine. Others say they are not. They say that too many pigs live in small, crowded spaces.

One farmer said that in the good old days, pigs lived outside. These smart animals had lots to do. They ran around in the forest and looked for food. Now many of them stay inside and get bored.

Soon, you pigs may get more than just footballs to play with. You may get homes that feel more like forests!

Still, you will never have as nice a home as Maggie Park's pets in Australia. Her three pigs live inside her house. At first the neighbors were mad. They said pigs were dirty. They said that Maggie should keep them outside. But government workers said no. They said pigs have the same rights as house pets.

Her pigs do not play with footballs. They like to watch TV all day! At night, they sleep in their own bedroom. Now that's a pig's life!

Scholastic Teaching Resources   **Grades 5-6**

1. **What is one reason farmers might not like the new law that says pigs need things to sniff?**

   _____

   _____

2. **How do you think toys will help pigs?**

   _____

   _____

3. **List one detail to support the conclusion that pigs become mean when kept in small, crowed places.**

   _____

   _____

4. **The author concludes that farm pigs may never have as nice a home as Maggie Park's pigs. Which statement does NOT support this conclusion.**
   - Ⓐ The Park pigs live in the house.
   - Ⓑ Neighbors think pigs are dirty.
   - Ⓒ The Park pigs watch TV.
   - Ⓓ The Park pigs sleep in their own bedroom.

5. **What can you conclude about farm animals from this passage?**
   - Ⓐ Soon all farm animals will be set free.
   - Ⓑ All farm animals should be treated like pets.
   - Ⓒ Farm animals are happiest in small, neat sties.
   - Ⓓ Farm animals have the right to be treated well.

Grades 5–6   **Scholastic Teaching Resources**

MY JOURNAL

October 14

Yesterday Dr. Hill put braces on my teeth. When she was finished, she walked me out to the front desk. She told Mrs. Pearl I would have to come back in two weeks to have my appliance checked. "Sounds like she put a washing machine in your mouth, doesn't it, Dan?" joked Mrs. Pearl. Then she gave me an appointment for 2:30 P.M. on October 28. Oh, well. I guess getting out of school early to see Dr. Hill will be one good thing about having braces.

Other things aren't so good. When I woke up this morning, my mouth really hurt. I couldn't eat my usual bowl of Crunchy Oats for breakfast. Too bad they don't get soggy in milk! I tried some peanut butter toast, and I couldn't even chew that. Finally Mom mashed a ripe banana and stirred in some milk and honey. My only other choice was a bowl of oatmeal, and *nothing* could get me to eat that stuff!

At school, my friends tried to be nice about my braces. Benny said he could hardly notice them unless I smiled. (Note to myself: Try not to smile too much.) Angel said they made me look more grown-up. And Keith told me I'm better off than he is. "At least you don't have the kind of braces that need rubber bands," he explained. "The rubber bands can come off and snap against the inside of your cheek."

Of course, Charlie Powers had mean things to say. First he called me Brace Face, and then he called me Metal Mouth. I ignored him, but he kept laughing and pointing. He didn't stop until Mrs. Fremont gave him one of her looks.

Right now, Dr. Hill's not sure how long I'll have to wear the braces. But it may be at least nine months. That seems like a long, long time.

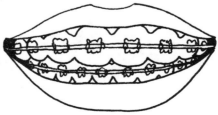

1. **Who do you think wrote this journal page?**

_____

2. **What do you think is Dr. Hill's job?**
- Ⓐ dentist
- Ⓑ eye doctor
- Ⓒ scientist
- Ⓓ animal doctor

3. **What do you think Dr. Hill was talking about when she used the word *appliance*?**

_____

4. **Which of these boys do you think wears braces?**
- Ⓐ Benny
- Ⓑ Angel
- Ⓒ Keith
- Ⓓ Charlie

5. **When Mrs. Fremont gave Charlie Powers a look, what do you think the look meant?**
- Ⓐ She had a job for him.
- Ⓑ He made a good joke.
- Ⓒ She was proud of him.
- Ⓓ He should be quiet.

29

Passage 17   Making Inferences and Predictions

What's for Lunch?

School Lunch Menu

MONDAY
May 26

School Holiday
Have a great holiday!

TUESDAY
May 27

Choice A
sandwich
baked potato slices
green beans

Choice B
vegetable soup
wheat crackers
carrot sticks

WEDNESDAY
May 28

Choice A
beef bites in gravy
dinner roll
corn

Choice B
cheese sandwich
French fries
tossed salad

THURSDAY
May 29

Choice A
chicken fingers
rice
peas

Choice B
pancakes
sliced peaches
corn

FRIDAY
May 30

Choice A
hot dog with bun
French fries
carrots

Choice B
cheese fries
fruit cup
tossed salad

lunch price: $1.50 (includes milk)
milk only: $.50

1. **Why doesn't the menu include lunch choices for Monday, May 26?**

   _____

   _____

2. **For whom do you think Choice B menus are made?**
   - Ⓐ people who don't eat meat
   - Ⓑ people who like breakfast
   - Ⓒ people who like beef
   - Ⓓ people who don't like to eat

3. **Why might you want to buy milk only?**
   - Ⓐ You might not like the drink served with Choice A.
   - Ⓑ You might not like the drink served with Choice B.
   - Ⓒ You might not be able to drink milk.
   - Ⓓ You might bring your own lunch, but not a drink.

4. **What drink is served with all Choice A and Choice B lunches?**

   _____

5. **Which of the following will probably be on the Choice B menu next week?**
   - Ⓐ cheese
   - Ⓑ fish
   - Ⓒ beef
   - Ⓓ chicken

   _____

   _____

   _____

Name _____ Date _____

MAKING A SCARECROW

*H*ow would you like your very own scarecrow? You can make one out of some old boards. You can use it to scare away birds in your garden. (*Scare* and *crow*—get it?). You can also put a scarecrow somewhere else, such as near your front door to give visitors a big surprise!

Here are some of the things you will need:

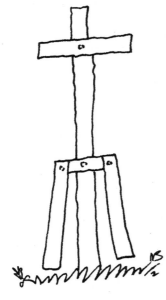

- a grown-up helper
- 3/4-inch boards as follows: one 5-feet long for a pole, three 16-inches long for the shoulders and arms, one 1-foot long for the hips, two 2-feet long for the legs
- a hammer and nails

- a shirt with long sleeves
- a long skirt
- boots
- gloves and safety pins
- an old pillowcase
- stuffing for the pillowcase
- two pieces of rope
- paint or felt-tipped pen
- a hat

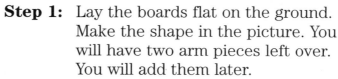

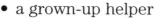

Step 1: Lay the boards flat on the ground. Make the shape in the picture. You will have two arm pieces left over. You will add them later.

Step 2: Ask a grown-up to nail the pieces together.

Step 3: Put the shirt over the scarecrow's shoulders. Ask a grown-up to nail the end of one arm piece to the shoulder. Let the sleeve fall back down so that it covers the arm board. Do the same with the other arm.

Step 4: Put the skirt around the scarecrow's hips. Tie it tight with rope.

Step 5: Stick the body into the ground.

Step 6: Put the boots under the skirt so it looks like it has feet.

Step 7: Pin the gloves to the sleeves.

Step 8: Fill the old pillowcase with stuffing such as hay, rags, or balled-up newspaper. Stick the open end over the neck. Then tie the open end with rope. Make a funny face on the pillow with paint or pen.

Step 9: Put a hat on its head.

---

1. **What should you and your grown-up helper do first?**
   - Ⓐ Lay the boards on the ground.
   - Ⓑ Put the shirt over the shoulders.
   - Ⓒ Nail the arm pieces.
   - Ⓓ Stuff the pillowcase.

2. **What should you do after you finish putting the shirt on the scarecrow?**

   _____

   _____

   _____

3. **What do you do right before you put the boots on the scarecrow?**

   _____

   _____

   _____

4. **Which step comes before you stuff the pillowcase?**
   - Ⓐ Paint a face on the pillowcase.
   - Ⓑ Pin gloves on the scarecrow.
   - Ⓒ Tie the end of the pillowcase.
   - Ⓓ Put a hat on the scarecrow.

5. **What is the last thing that you do?**

   _____

Passage 19   Story Elements

Am I a Robot?

Shawn and Pat were brothers. Twelve-year-old Shawn was always up to something. He liked to play jokes. He did not always do his homework on time. Sometimes he "forgot" to wash the dishes. His bedroom was a mess!

Pat, on the other hand, had always behaved like an angel.

"What a wonderful baby!" his mother would say. "He never cried!"

Pat was never a terrible two-year-old. His teachers always said, "What a joy it is to have Pat in class! He is never any trouble! He is so different from his brother.

Pat did not think much about how great he was until one day when he was watching *Mostly Martin*. In the show, a new boy had moved to town.

"He is strange," said Martin. "He never gets into trouble. He does everything he's supposed to do. Everyone thinks he is perfect. He must be a robot!"

He went to find Shawn, who was playing with a frog on the kitchen table. "Am I a robot?" he asked.

"Of course not," said Shawn as he went outside.

Pat thought hard. Robots were machines. They looked like people, but they were not really alive. They always followed orders. How would you know that you were one?

Pat decided to ask his parents. After all, they must know.

He asked at dinner. His father laughed. "Sure!" he said, "and it's time to change your batteries!" He jumped up and ran to the tool drawer.

"Dad's just kidding!" said Pat's mother. "Of course you are not a robot, Pat. You are our son."

Pat felt better for a while. But that night he began to worry again. Of course his mother said he was real. Nice mothers would not tell their sons they are robots!

Pat crept down the hall to Shawn's room. Shawn was playing a computer game in the dark. This was against the rules.

"How can I know for *sure* that I am not a robot?" asked Pat.

For once, Shawn did not play a joke on his little brother. He could tell that Pat was really worried. After all, Pat was only six.

"What makes you think that you *are* one?" he said.

"People always say I am perfect," answered Pat. "But only robots are!"

Shawn smiled to himself. He knew exactly what to do.

The next morning, his mother opened Pat's bedroom door. "Time for school!"

"No," said Pat.

His mother was surprised. This had never happened before. "You have to."

"No!" yelled Pat. He kicked his feet and rolled around in bed.

"Patrick" his mother said in a loud voice. "Get out of bed this minute!"

Pat gave a few more kicks. He felt very silly. He was also happy. No robot would ever act this way. He was a real boy. Now he knew for sure.

1. What is the setting for most of this story?

_____

_____

2. How does Pat's problem begin?

- Ⓐ His brother calls him a robot.
- Ⓑ He gets in trouble for making noise in school.
- Ⓒ He sees a TV show with a perfect boy.
- Ⓓ He plays a computer game one night.

3. How does Pat solve his problem?

_____

_____

4. What is the setting at the end of the story?

_____

5. What lesson does Pat learn in this story?

_____

_____

Passage 20   Fact and Opinion

Really Big Hair

About two hundred years ago, French women wore their hair in a very strange way. Queen Marie Antoinette started the fashion. The first step for a woman fixing her hair was to put a small pillow or a wire frame on top of her head. Next the woman pinned fake hair in with her real hair. Then she brushed all the hair—real and fake—up over the pillow or frame. It looked as if she had lots of BIG hair.

To keep the hair in place, the woman covered it with sticky wax. Then she powdered her hair. Most of the time she used white powder, or sometimes pink. Then she put flowers and feathers on this big, sticky, powdered pile. Women with these hairdos looked very silly.

It took a lot of work to keep their hair in place. Women often had to sleep sitting up. This was silly! Also, people did not wash their hair very often back then. Because of this, sometimes bugs lived in the women's tall hairdos. The bugs may have thought all that wax tasted great!

A big hairdo made it hard for women to get around. Sometimes they could not even fit through low doors. Life was not much fun!

In the late 1700s, only rich women could pay for fancy hairdos. Poor people could hardly pay for food. Life in France was unfair. Soon a revolution started. The French people got rid of their king and queen. After that, it was dangerous to look rich. That was the end of the big, powdered hair.

1. Which sentence is an opinion from the first paragraph?
- Ⓐ French women wore their hair in a very strange way.
- Ⓑ Queen Marie Antoinette started the fashion.
- Ⓒ Next the woman pinned fake hair in with her real hair.
- Ⓓ Then she brushed all the hair.

2. Which sentence from the second paragraph is an opinion?
- Ⓐ The woman covered it with sticky wax.
- Ⓑ Then she powdered her hair.
- Ⓒ Most of the time she used white powder.
- Ⓓ Women with these hairdos looked very silly.

3. Which sentence in the last three paragraphs states a fact?
- Ⓐ This was silly!
- Ⓑ The bugs may have thought all that wax tasted great!
- Ⓒ Life was not much fun!
- Ⓓ Soon a revolution started.

36

Passage 21   Cause and Effect

Extreme Jason

Jason turned off the TV. He had been watching the X Games. Athletes from all over the world were competing in the most amazing sports. A girl climbed a wall of ice. A man raced down a snowy mountain on a bicycle.

Just then his grandmother walked into the room with some cookies. Jason took one and sighed.

"I want to be extreme," he said.

"You are!" she laughed.

"I mean I want to be an extreme athlete," said Jason.

"Well," she said, "surfing is out. We are hundreds of miles from the ocean. We don't live near any mountains, so you can't ski or snowboard. I guess it will have to be skateboarding."

"Would you really let me? You always worry about me being safe!" said Jason.

"You will have to follow some rules," said his grandmother. "You can only ride in the park—never on the streets. You have to promise to wear a helmet. If you hurt yourself too much, I have the right to take your board away. Is it a deal?"

"You bet!" Jason was so excited that he jumped up. Cookie crumbs flew everywhere.

A week later he had a board and a helmet. He had pads for his knees and elbows.

On Saturday, his grandmother dropped him off near the park. "I'll be up the street at the library," she said. "Meet me there when you've had enough."

"OK. Thanks," Jason said as he got out of the car. He was happy to have a grandmother who let him try new things.

Kids in the park were whizzing up and down the ramps. They flew into the air and landed as easily as birds. They skated backwards and spun circles in the air.

Jason just stood there. When he watched the *X Games*, he felt like he was doing the tricks himself. But watching these kids up close, he knew that none of it was going to be easy. He wished he could just walk by as if he were going somewhere else.

"Hey, Jason!" yelled a kid from school.

"Hey!" Jason's voice sounded funny because he was scared.

Slowly he put on his pads. Very slowly he carried his board to the ramp. Taking a deep breath, he put his right foot on the board. He kicked off with his left foot. For a few seconds he glided along, just waiting to fall. Then he came to a stop. Kicking off again, he waited for the worst to happen. Again, he stayed up. The third time he kicked, lost his balance, and fell hard on his left knee.

It hurt, but it was no big deal! Why had he been so scared? Now he felt calm because things had gone wrong, and he was fine!

Next time he kicked off harder and went faster and farther.

"Excellent!" yelled a girl as she passed him.

"Extreme!" laughed Jason to himself. "Not quite."

1. Why does his grandmother suggest skateboarding instead of surfing, skiing, or snowboarding?

    Ⓐ They don't live near the ocean or mountains.

    Ⓑ She used to skateboard as a child.

    Ⓒ She thinks water and snow sports are dangerous.

    Ⓓ Skateboarding is the hardest.

2. Why is Jason surprised when his grandmother mentions skateboarding?

    Ⓐ She wants him to try other sports instead.

    Ⓑ She always worries about his safety.

    Ⓒ She wants him to work harder in school.

    Ⓓ She never wants him to have a good time.

3. Why does Jason jump off the couch?

    Ⓐ He wants more cookies.

    Ⓑ He's going out to play.

    Ⓒ He's excited about skateboarding.

    Ⓓ He's angry at his grandmother.

4. At the park, why can't Jason just walk past the skateboarders and leave?

_____

_____

5. Why does Jason feel better after he falls and hurts his knee?

_____

_____

Grades 5-6

Passage 22   Drawing Conclusions

MOM GOES ON STRIKE

Belleville, Illinois—On October 7, Michelle Tribout climbed into her kids' tree house. It was a good place, she decided, for a mother to go on strike. Mrs. Tribout, 36, was tired of having her three children talk back to her. She was tired of driving them everywhere without thanks and doing more than her share of the work around the house. Until things changed, Mrs. Tribout was going to stay up in the tree.

Mrs. Tribout's strike got her kids' attention, of course. But that's not all that happened. Word of the fed-up mother spread. Before long, a camera crew from television's *Today Show* pulled into the Tribouts' yard. Now people all across America were going to find out about the kids who drove their mother up a tree.

"On Strike: No Cooking, No Cleaning, No Rides"

As the cameras rolled, the three Tribout kids stood with their father near the tree house. Katie Couric, the *Today Show* host, had a question for them. "What do you think about your mom on strike in that tree house?" she asked.

"I am kind of embarrassed," said Misty.

"I'm really shocked," said Joseph. "I did not think it would go this far."

Rachel added, "I think she's pretty weird."

But Mrs. Tribout had made her point. If the kids wanted her back, they knew what they had to do. When the TV crew left, Misty, Rachel, and Joseph went into their house and got busy. Not long after that, Mrs. Tribout climbed down from the tree and went back to being a mom.

---

1. How did people across America find out about the Tribout kids?

_____

_____

2. What was Mrs. Tribout doing while Katie Couric talked to her children?

    Ⓐ sitting in the tree house   Ⓒ driving her car

    Ⓑ watching TV   Ⓓ resting in bed

3. When the Tribout kids went back into the house, what do you think they did?

    Ⓐ talked back to their mother   Ⓒ did some chores

    Ⓑ played games   Ⓓ read the newspaper

Passage 23   Main Idea and Details

ANDREA DORIA SURVIVOR

New York, NY
July 25, 1956

Word has just come of a terrible tragedy—and good luck. Both happened at the same time.

Just a few hours ago, the Italian ship *Andrea Doria* was steaming through thick fog, toward the city of New York. Captain Piero Calamai kept watch. He knew that many other ships were nearby. He should have slowed down because of the fog but he decided not to. He wanted to arrive on time the next morning.

At about 11:00 P.M., another ship, the *S.S. Stockholm*, suddenly crashed into the *Andrea Doria*. The bow of the *Stockholm* cut right through the side of the *Andrea Doria*. It made a huge hole in the Italian ship. Some people were badly hurt. Others fell into the sea. But one girl was saved by the *Stockholm*!

Linda Morgan was just fourteen years old. She lived in Spain with her mother, her stepfather, and her little sister. She was going to visit her father in New York.

Linda had loved the trip. She was excited about seeing her father. She had fun swimming in the ship's three outdoor pools. She liked the delicious Italian food, and she looked forward to having dinner with the Captain on the last night at sea.

The Captain did not sit at his table that night, though. He was busy guiding the ship through the fog. Linda did not get to talk to him.

When Linda went to bed, everything seemed fine. Her mother turned out the lights. Linda talked to her little sister. She thought about seeing her father the next morning.

What happened next was a terrible surprise. Linda woke up not knowing where she was. She was not in her bed. When she called to her family, no one answered. She was in great pain. Both her knees were broken!

Linda had been saved by an amazing accident. When the *Stockholm* made a hole in the side of the *Andrea Doria*, it lifted Linda out of her bed. She landed on the deck of the *Stockholm* instead of falling into the ocean. A sailor heard her cries and found her.

Right now, this miracle girl is in the hospital. She is expected to get better. We do not yet know where the rest of her family is. Her father is at her side, glad that his little girl was saved. The *Andrea Doria* lies under the waves at the bottom of the sea.

1. What is the main idea of Paragraph 2?

    Ⓐ Fog filled the air around New York City.

    Ⓑ The *Andrea Doria* was steaming toward New York.

    Ⓒ The captain wanted to arrive on time.

    Ⓓ Captain Piero Calamai kept watch.

2. Write one detail from the passage to support the idea that Linda Morgan enjoyed the trip to New York.

_____

_____

_____

3. Why didn't the captain sit at Linda's table that night?

_____

_____

_____

4. Write one detail about how Linda was saved.

_____

_____

5. Which is a main idea of this article?

    Ⓐ Edward Morgan was a radio broadcaster.

    Ⓑ Linda Morgan lived in Spain with her mother and stepfather.

    Ⓒ After her mother turned out the lights, Linda talked to her sister.

    Ⓓ Linda Morgan was saved by an amazing accident.

Writing Prompt: **On a separate piece of paper, write in your own words about what happened to Linda Morgan on the** *Andrea Doria.*

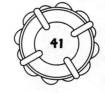

Passage 24   Fact and Opinion

Welcome to Our Web Site!

AFTER SCHOOL FUN

at Chester Elementary School

March 10–May 23 (There will be no classes during spring vacation, April 14–18.)

"After School Fun" begins at 3:15. Pick up is at 4:15. You MUST be picked up each day by 4:30 at the latest. After 4:30 the school is locked. All classes are free, but for some you'll need special supplies. Sign up by March 3. Classes fill quickly! This is a great way to fill the time between school and dinner!

Beading Teacher: Kirsten Olafsdattir. In this class, you can make a beautiful beaded bracelet. You'll also learn how to put together cute friendship pins and hair-clips. Beading is fun and easy. Anyone can learn! (The teacher can tell you where to buy supplies.) Fridays, Art Room

Games Your Grandparents Played Teacher: Susanna O'Neill. This class will show you how children played long ago. You'll roll marbles and pick up jacks. You'll jump rope and play running games. You'll learn counting rhymes. The games your grandparents played were really fun! Wear comfortable clothes. Mondays, Gym

¡Spanish, Sí! Teacher: Juan Alvarado. Did you know that Spanish is spoken by more than 17 million Americans? After a few weeks with Señor Alvarado, you'll be able to talk about the weather. You'll be able to name the people in your family. You'll be able to name clothes and animals. For the last class, you will go to a real Mexican restaurant and order a meal in Spanish! Mexican food is truly delicious! Tuesdays, Library

Tae Kwon Do Teacher: Nina Malpas. Tae Kwon Do is a Korean martial art. Tae Kwon Do is better than just a sport. It teaches you to move beautifully. It teaches you to believe in yourself and have respect for others. Tae Kwon Do is fun, but it is more than that. It can make you into a better person. Nina Malpas is the best Tae Kwon Do teacher around. You'll love her class. Wear loose, comfortable clothing. Thursdays, Gym

1. Which sentence is an opinion?

    Ⓐ "After School Fun" begins at 3:15.

    Ⓑ After 4:30 the school is locked.

    Ⓒ All classes are free, but for some you'll need special supplies.

    Ⓓ This is a great way to fill the time between school and dinner!

2. Which sentence states a fact about the beading class?

    Ⓐ You can make a beautiful beaded bracelet.

    Ⓑ Anyone can learn!

    Ⓒ Beading is fun and easy.

    Ⓓ The teacher can tell you where to buy supplies.

3. Look at the description of "Games Your Grandparents Played." Write the sentence that states an opinion from the description.

_____

_____

_____

4. Find the description of "¡Spanish, Sí!" Write one fact and one opinion from the description.

Fact: _____

Opinion: _____

5. Read the description of the Tae Kwon Do class. Is this description mostly fact or mostly opinion? Tell why you think so.

_____

_____

_____

Passage 25 Comparing and Contrasting

A Common Language?

Do you think Great Britain and the United States are alike? Winston Churchill once joked that the people of Britain and the people of America are separated only by their language. Do you think that is true? The British and the Americans both speak English as the official language. However, each uses some different words. We Americans are similar to the British. After all, our country was once owned by Great Britain, so we have a lot in common. But there are many differences between us.

Great Britain has a king or queen, and the leader of the government is the Prime Minister. The United States has no kings or queens. Our leader is the President.

Both the British and Americans have long measured using pounds and ounces, pints, quarts, and gallons. Both use miles, yards, and feet. Our money is different, though. The British use pounds and pence. Americans use dollars and cents.

Driving in a car is very different in England. They drive on the left side of the road. We drive on the right. What we call the hood of the car, the British call the "bonnet." British cars run on "petrol," which we call gasoline.

In our everyday lives, we do many of the same things as the British. But we describe them differently. A young mother here might push a baby in a baby carriage. A British mom pushes a "pram." The British watch the "telly," while we watch TV. We like to eat French fries, but the British call them "chips." Many people in England eat "bangers and mash." We call them sausages and mashed potatoes. Millions of Americans drink coffee, but most British prefer tea.

So we are different in many ways. But we stay friendly anyway.

1. **The British and the Americans both _____.**
   - Ⓐ use English as their official language
   - Ⓑ have the same exact words for things
   - Ⓒ have countries on the same continent
   - Ⓓ live in small countries

2. **What is an important difference between the governments of the two countries?**

   _____

   _____

3. **The British and the Americans both use _____.**
   - Ⓐ dollars and cents
   - Ⓑ pounds and pence
   - Ⓒ pints and gallons
   - Ⓓ meters and liters

4. **What is the main difference in road travel between the two countries?**

   _____

   _____

   _____

5. **What is the American name for "chips?"**

   _____

   Writing Prompt: **Do you think the British and Americans are mostly alike or mostly different? On a separate piece of paper, explain your answer.**

Answer Key

1. Snow Day

1. B
2. A
3. go sledding

2. Hopping Around the World

1. Examples: In Escargot, no puck is used; the pattern is in the shape of a snail.
2. It has the days of the week instead of numbers.
3. D
4. B
5. A

3. Problems Solved—By Kids!

1. C
2. B
3. Examples: Suzanna lived about 100 years later. She became an inventor at a much younger age.

4. Squirrel in a Life Jacket

1. She is a funny sight.
2. Always wear a life jacket when boating or water-skiing.
3. A
4. C
5. the crowds laughing and cheering for her squirrel on water skis

5. Don't Bake These Cookies!

1. sugar, butter, and milk
2. C
3. Let the cookies cool for 30 minutes.

6. A Brother in the Band

1. Aaron Carter is a singer and a brother of Nick Carter's.
2. B
3. C

7. A Fascinating Fish

1. B
2. Examples: It hides in plants and grasses; it changes colors to blend with its surroundings.
3. She puts the eggs into the male's pouch.
4. Examples: Places where they once lived have been filled with land; many are caught for aquariums.
5. D

8. A Delicious Mistake

1. C
2. A
3. A
4. The candy makers were smart. They realized chocolate chips would sell well because chocolate chip cookies are so good.
5. homemade and hot from the oven

Writing Prompt: Answers will vary.

9. The Amazing Angie

1. A
2. D
3. B
4. She is going to use it as a crystal ball for telling fortunes.
5. A

10. The Show Must Go On!

1. a doctor's office
2. She broke her leg two weeks before a dance performance.
3. D

11. The Last Day

1. He walked into the classroom with a CD player.
2. Mr. Brinks plugged in the CD player and turned it on.
3. B
4. Mr. Brinks dropped the balls on the floor and announced recess.
5. D

12. What's in a Name?

1. C
2. Look in a name book.
3. A

13. Ask Daisy

1. B
2. Vic is kind and funny and is always there to help Leon.
3. C

14. Letter From the New World

1. A
2. They eat fruit, which makes their lips purple.
3. They had eaten all the fruit they had picked.
4. B
5. C

15. Piggy Heaven

1. The pigs' pens will be harder to clean.
2. They will play with the toy instead of getting bored and hurting others.
3. They begin to bite one another.
4. B
5. D

16. My Journal

1. Dan
2. A
3. braces
4. C
5. D

17. What's for Lunch?

1. Monday is a holiday; school is closed.
2. A
3. D
4. milk
5. A

18. Making a Scarecrow

1. A
2. Put the skirt on the scarecrow and tie it.
3. Stick the scarecrow's body into the ground.
4. B
5. Put a hat on the scarecrow.

19. Am I a Robot?

1. Pat and Shawn's house
2. C
3. He acts naughtily, or he breaks some rules. This proves he is a real boy, since robots always do as they are told.
4. Pat's bedroom
5. Pat learns that he does not have to be perfect.

20. Really Big Hair

1. A
2. D
3. D

21. Extreme Jason

1. A
2. B
3. C
4. He is carrying a skateboard.
5. He realizes that falling is not a big deal.

22. Mom Goes on Strike

1. People found out by watching them on the *Today Show* on TV.
2. A
3. C

23. *Andrea Doria* Survivor

1. B
2. Examples: She was excited about seeing her father; she had fun swimming; she enjoyed the food.
3. He was busy guiding the ship through the fog.
4. Examples: When the *Stockholm* made a hole in the *Andrea Doria*, it lifted Linda out of her bed; she landed on the deck of the *Stockholm* instead of falling into the ocean; a sailor heard her cries and found her.
5. D

Writing Prompt: Answers will vary.

24. After School Fun

1. D
2. D
3. The games your grandparents played were really fun!
4. Example—Fact: More than 17 million Americans speak Spanish. Opinion: Mexican food is truly delicious!
5. This description is mostly opinion. Almost every sentence has an opinion word, such as *better, beautifully, fun,* and *best.*

25. A Common Language?

1. A
2. Great Britain has a king or queen, and a prime minister, while the U.S. has a president.
3. C
4. The British drive on the left side of the road; Americans drive on the right.
5. French fries

Writing Prompt: Answers will vary.